Love & Cro

JOHN LINDLEY

SPM Publications
London

SPM Publications
Unit 136, 113-115 George Lane, South Woodford,
London E18 1AB, United Kingdom
www.spmpublications.com

First published in Great Britain by SPM Publications – an imprint of
Sentinel Writing & Publishing Company in September 2018.

ISBN 978-0-9935035-9-7

Sentinel Writing & Publishing Company is a style of SPM Publications Ltd.

Cover Art – "The Death of Man" by Mark Sheeky ©2018
www.marksheeky.com

Book Design & Typography by Nnorom Azuonye
Set in Garamond 9 – 16 points

For Jane

and in fond memory of
Anthony David Crump
1958 – 2017

Other books by John Lindley

Dylan Thomas: Embers & Sparks (Riverdane, 2014)
Screen Fever (Pinewood, 2012)
The Casting Boat (Headland, 2009)
House of Wonders (Riverdane, 2008)
Cheshire Rising (Cheshire County Council, 2005)
Scarecrow Crimes (New Hope International, 2002)
Stills from November Campaigns (Tarantula, 1998)
Cages and Fields (1982)
Pacific Envelope (1976)

Acknowledgements are due to the editors of the following magazines and anthologies in which some of these poems first appeared: *Adrift, from Belsize to Havana*; *Antiphon*; *Book Box*; *Citizen 32*; *Fifty Ways to Fly*; *Lest We Forget*; *Obsessed with Pipework*; *Orbis*; *Poems for Grenfell Tower*; *Sentinel Literary Quarterly*; *The Interpreter's House*; *The Painter's Quarry*.

Initiation won 1st prize in the Manchester Cathedral Poetry Competition.

Resurrection won 3nd prize in the Provocations Poetry Competition.

John 'Hangman' Ellis won 3nd prize in the *Sentinel Literary Quarterly* Poetry Competition.

The Woman who gave birth to a Ghost won 3nd prize in the Wirral Festival of Firsts Competition

Inheritance was commended in the Sentinel *Literary Quarterly* Poetry Competition.

God's Library was commended in the Staffordshire Libraries Poetry Competition.

Contents

LOVE & CROSSBONES

The Woman Who Gave Birth to a Ghost

Perhaps it was the distractedness of his lovemaking that night –
heart not in it and a mouth that went through the motions –
but for nine months his wife bled to the calendar,
stayed toned, kept down her breakfasts.
The ease of the birth surprised no-one: a vapour
from the womb shaping up to a boy decidedly underweight.
Something not right about the skin.
Grey as an eraser, he took to his feeds for novelty's sake:
x-ray of milk down a pale windpipe in a vain search for bones.
He never slept. Whether in his cot or between parents
in the twin plot of the marriage bed. He never slept.
Even at that age he dreamt, wide awake, of the substance of death.
Clothes became a problem. It was like trying to dress smoke.
Slender as a wraith said the neighbours.
All that time his parents awaited his first word, or his last.
He passed through childhood, puberty, walls and locked doors;
drifted through his teens; made nothing of himself.
Hard to say what became of him; left before his parents though.
Never a word. Young 'uns can be like that sometimes.

Beware of the Poem

Although
this dog of mine
is not a poem
this poem of mine
is a dog.
No,
not a dog poem.
Well, it is
but it isn't
a poem
about dogs
rather
it's a poem
that circles
seemingly pointlessly clockwise
then
anti-clockwise
before falling
on the same bed
of a page it started with.
It sleeps in the drawer
of my desk
and dreams visibly:
twitching,
making strange noises.
I let it out.
It runs wild,
stops just once
to stare at nothing
on the ceiling.
Good Boy, I tell it.
Reassured, it follows me out,
walks nearly to heel,
barks loudly
at my neighbour's poem.

A Short History of My Father

Short he was, five-one or two
or thereabouts, strong with a slight paunch,
like Napoleon, I suppose, but with a kinder mouth
and with no forward-looking forelock
when his hairline went south.

Today I recall the short men,
no less memorable than the tall:
Toulouse Lautrec, Mickey Rooney,
Paul Simon and some of the sweetest ball
players I've ever seen – Price
and Henderson on County's wings –
running rings round visiting backs
at Edgeley Park. Thinking back,

Dad didn't do rings. He held the nap hand for class,
was dapper in a suit, did weddings with panache,
but not wedding rings. Hated wearing his.
Didn't do flash. Cuff-links his only bling.

I wear it now – ring finger, right hand – perfect fit
but Dad was so unenamoured of it
I'm surprised he didn't stick his hand
in his coat like Napoleon to hide that gold band.
Sort of thing he might have done.
At least that's what I figure.
Stood there posing. A man like Napoleon
only bigger.

Over and Done

Well, it's all over now bar the shouting,
Dad would say every Christmas morning
as the last gift was undressed and revealed.
Mum's magnificent dinner gave the lie
to that, so did the corny paper hats,
crackers, Mackeson bottles and wine.
Stuffed as turkeys, I played, our Dad napped,
our Mum did whatever mums did back then
till tea-time. Then the cat napped, my brother
and sister made tracks, Dad drank a Whisky Mac
at day's end.
        At day's end, think I'll go like that:
crackers, played out, well and truly stuffed,
one last Whisky Mac. Goodnight gently,
perhaps, or all over bar the shouting.

The Malleable God

I shovelled this shape from down deep,
soul searched and strip-mined,
bundled and tugged it through the factory gates,
hung it on three coat hooks
while I got the furnace hot.

I forged an idea of omnipotence
in a smithy of my fancy,
poured in the requisite radiance
and hammered him into usefulness.

He was huge and holy when I finished him.
As he cooled, my workshop walls
grew hot as sin.
I wheeled him into the night
and the door frame trembled at his passing.

I saddled him as he was stirring
and, as the sky divided into dawn,
he split too; forked into the Holy Trinity.
I chose the Son and rode him like my luck.

I was thrown before breakfast,
hoofbeats and hymns growing fainter,
three Gods shrinking in the wilderness.
I walked all the way home.

A promise though to meet again at sunset
to talk about old times: the Father
at the foundry gates when all was still new,
the Son crucified on three hooks
and the Ghost huffing in and out of the bellows
like the beliefs that you can never nail down.

Kids' Stuff

None of our games made the Olympics:
the furthest spit, the unblinked eye,
the highest piss up the wall.

Knuckles didn't get in
nor *Spin the Bottle, Kiss Chase*
or *Chinese Burns*.

No, they fanny about instead
with bikes, hurdles, javelins and discus
and pussyfoot around our games

like that chicken kid in Class 3
would pussyfoot around his unstabbed fingers,
delicately, with a too slow compass.

Paid in Full

MacDonald, Routledge, Espley, Jones, Morris,
Lomas, Trueman, Cope, Hodgkinson and Ball.
Barnett, Parker, Hill, Dean, Rutland, Norris,
Robinson, Mountford, Sproston, Blake and Hall.

For the widows and orphans to come –
The Chronicle Shilling Fund. Please donate.
And from distant France an insistent drum
thrums in the hearts of men at Glory's gate.

Join the colours. Fly the flag. Share in the fighting.
The cause is vague but (for now) the choice is free
and the sound of a rifle's more exciting
than that of a machine in a factory.

Taylor (Joseph), Turner (Frank) Carney (James).
"Here, Sir." Each schoolboy with arm erect.
Now, different uniforms but the same names
barked out. The reply, "Yes, Sir. Present and correct."

But a country's flag protects no-one from harm.
A bitter truth that many learn too late.
Death is no respecter of uniform,
it is random, cold, indiscriminate.

Now Walter Ashley, Samuel Jesse Wright –
all those who joined 'The Great Majority' –
march from light to dark, from dark to light,
carved in stone and on our faint memory.

A bell in St. Stephen's rings. Shadows
fall on Lawton Street. Answers are sought.
What price glory? A shilling for the widows,
the orphans. A penny for your thoughts.

Fay Wray

There's no-one today quite like Fay Wray,
once Kong had delicately stripped her
with a finger until her ripped dress slipped
toward censorship I've thought how careful

one would need to be, if one were he, not
to bruise that near naked hip, cut that lip
with a fingernail the size of a spade.
Oh, how she writhed in her tininess,

clinging on to her leather trapeze
when only her scream was huge, the petals
of her torn white dress falling soundless as snow.
And one could see why he was smitten,

encountering the only delicious treat
he'd ever seen and chosen not to eat.
All other 'love at first sights' surely pale
against this hairy courtier's for his pale

prize. His eyes near as wide as his smile.
he perched and worshipped her in the church
of his hand, on the altar of his palm –
no sacrificial lamb to the slaughter

but a pearl of flesh, a working miniature,
the tiny mechanism of her crooked arm
no longer shielding her eyes from his glare
and the only movement, the insects

through the darkest jungles of his soft fur.
Well, all's well that ends well goes the play
but unrequited love rarely does;
it stays unrequited and nothing slakes

its heartache but a stammer of blood
as from the bullets from a bi-plane
and the fall, not from a state of grace,
but from a man-made rock to a harder place.

And Fay Wray? She remains just a scream away
in the house of the head on the street,
horizontal. And in my horizontal
dreaming head, decades and decades away,

she lays her pretty projected cheek
on my chest, a chest unriddled by bullets,
unriddled by doubt as to who would hold
the upper hand for her hand – me or Kong.

Another Language

The doctor says there's an imbalance in me
that's causing anxiety: the left side of my brain
is not talking to my right foot (or something).
Medics, like accountants, like mechanics,
like computer buffs have their own language.
They know the Latin for larynx (if larynx isn't Latin)
and how to unravel the tangled wiring
of the nervous system and string it into words.
Only for our sakes and understanding
do they dumb down – *Athlete's Foot,* the *Common Cold* –
and even then not always. The name
of my medication has all the letters of the alphabet
bar a couple (and not the ones you'd think).
I swallow the lexicon three times a day after meals,
sense my body mend and mesh, my energy levels rise.
The quick brown fox jumps over the lazy dog
but only in layman's terms.

Annunciation

You come with your bad news ticking in your mouth,
fan the giant brag of your wings,
open your 'nothing up my sleeve' hands
and magic her a gift that must be paid for.

You find her where she'd not be found –
in the shadow of betrothal,
declare her the chosen vessel for the chosen one
and lodge a weight in her womb that grows like rumour.

Ever after she might tell this tale,
truthfully, sheepishly to all who'll listen:
how feathers fell from the sky in the shape of a man,
how he spoke a seed into her unopened sex,

how, after the gentlest, most shocking of rapes,
he left the scene of the crime
letting the white light of witchcraft
confetti down on her from above.

Hangman's Manual

Not a knack but a careful computing
of height, weight and the distance of the drop.
All these criteria must be put in
place, so to ensure a quick death – the snap

of the spinal cord. Overestimate
and decapitation's the possible
outcome. Then again, underestimate
and the victim's survival's probable.

Note, please, the Legal Requirement that three
cervical vertebrae must be fractured
in order for the spinal cord to be
snapped clean. Remember that once they're captured

these murderers have no claim to mercy.
That does not mean, however, that they should
not be shown manners, common courtesy –
a meal, a curt *Good morning* and a hood.

Condemned

Unfinished, he sees only a Carroll
conundrum coupled with an Emily
Dickinson poem taking shape. Once he
has had his head drawn in, that is. Until

then he's on tiptoe at pencil tip,
watching his gallows go up: horizontal,
vertical, horizontal, diagonal
and that absurd stubby sliver of rope.

Up to that point his life's simply filler.
He plays a waiting game whilst the letter
of the law is applied. His sentence broken
only when light dawns and the h_ngm_n's beaten.

John 'Hangman' Ellis

With thirty years of trapdoor and drop
to his name, John Ellis divided his throat
(ironic or what?) with a clean sweep;
turned to the razor when life's knot

got too tight. Not for him chair, rope
and the dead man's dance. Not for him
the wrench, sway and dangle. The quick rip
was good enough to quit life's grim

joke. John Ellis, spur of the moment, saw
no time for reflection or final note,
lost it in that moment – barbershop floor
to his cheekbone, red reservoir at his throat.

'Barber'. Let's not forget that. 'Barber'.
So maybe that cut-throat was apt after all.
The hanging and roadshow years over,
hearing his and the Nation's depression call.

Did it ever occur to him before,
I wonder, when lathering that blade
on a leather strap? Who knows for sure
how such impossible choices get made:

asp or gas, whisky and pills, arsenic
or Lysol, train track, river or pond
and – my God! All those slick blade and bullet-
in-the-mouth bargains with the beyond?

Either or

I believe I am destined forever
to be unable to distinguish
between swallows and swifts,
moorhens and coots
and practice and practise.

I forget as quickly as I learn
the differing tails, beaks, consonants
and the tricks to remember them by.

I knew someone
who was the same with numbers,
who saw 3s as 8s even with his glasses on
and who lost in his head and his mouth
the registration of his just nicked car
the moment he dialled 666 for the police.

We're neither of us stupid (I like to think),
we just have these things that riddle us
that many others cope with.
We're rather like coots (or moorhens)
in practice flight, or young swifts
executing their perfect figure 3s
in the night swallowed sky.

Something About Knives

There's something about a knife in the hand
of the non-violent – the dagger, combat,
bayonet, trench, stiletto and hunting knife –

and something too about knives – the butcher's,
skinning, boning, carving, bread – in the hands
of those who never enter the kitchen.

There are those who love knives beyond their use.
They hold the throwing knife but will not throw,
the oyster knife but will not pry, the cobbler's

knife but will not mend. I am one of them.
Mostly. True, I've trimmed Axminster, shaved hair,
held and used a skeleton to cut cheese,

run the opener the length of a letter
to spill good news or bad (never, so far,
removed a stone from a horse's hoof) but

for the aesthete knives exceed their functions.
I've barely ever seen one on display
that I didn't long to fold, hold or own,

handles plastic and bone honed to my palm,
Victrinox and Swiss slipped in my pocket,
clasps closed and belt-clipped, shapely scout knives sheathed.

Look where they lie: climbing and camping shops,
laid proudly out in glass cubes like trinkets
in Tiffany's, gems in Hatton Garden

or in seedier surrounds seen nestling
in with camouflage and guns, serrated
blades for the gutting of fish (or who knows what?)

The shiv, the shank won't do, the inmates' knife
crudely made, crudely used would miss the point.
It's all in the craft, the shape and the weight,

the swivel and lock, the tactile, the touch;
all in the glint and the steel, the handle,
the edge that has the edge over all tools,

weapons, means of murder and sacrifice
that man has made. Man-made for machismo,
maybe, but finely, elegantly so.

Pyow Pyow

He took the same route as the 92 bus,
rode the narrow prairie of the A6
between Stockport and Longsight
on a too small bike, fired air bullets
from his loaded fingers at those he rolled by.

Pyow! Pyow!

Fifty? Fifty-five? With his Colt 45 digits
discharging painless death and liberty,
steering one-handed past the biscuit works,
the junk emporium, Albert St. junction,
The Crown, he's gabardined and peak-capped,
bottle-bottom glasses with lenses
the colour of Manchester weather
he pedalled harsh justice to all.

Pyow! Pyow!

We christened him after his gunfire.

It was decades ago but today,
stalled at the lights, I exchanged shots
through my front windscreen with a boy
in the back seat of the car in front
and remembered.

Pyow! Pyow!

I think I even said it. To the boy. To myself.
To the memory of the wobbling avenger.
To each and every pedestrian he shot
who only died laughing.

Foss Moves House

Lear's cat tracks a parallel universe,
soft foots through the familiar
and hangs from vermilion curtains
like a cat.

The replica that architects erect –
room for room and stair for stair –
is nearly there but misses by a whisker.

Foss sits on the sill and grooms his blunt tail.

Through the glass the same
saucer-like moon laps the house,
the same sun but everything else
out there has changed.

In here too – something not quite right,
something strange; strange as that same guitar
in the corner, the one that owls play,
if only in poems.

Edward Lear was reputedly so devoted to his cat, Foss, that, on moving, he had his new house built as a replica of the old to make the move less traumatic for his pet.

2016

So it was the year of the body count;
every year is but these were famous bodies:
movie stars, a Starman, a poet of song,
authors, comedians. The nobodies

didn't make it to our screens or the pages –
not of the Nationals anyway – their obits
populating only local papers.
The others were up there before the tits

on page 3 if pop stars, with authors buried
deep inside, at least as far as Tabloids went.
The Broadsheets took death more seriously,
gave due reverence – page after page spent

on biography and on legacy
in a belated appreciation
whilst we jammed up social media in
a mass mourning mass across the nation.

Meanwhile, in the background but not backlit,
all those private deaths were racking up too.
From January to December they
fell like flies, as the unremarkable do,

noticed and remarked upon by none
but family, friends, fellow workmates, the few.

Double Talk

Safety measures are firmly in place.
In the event of fire – 'Stay put'. We remain firmly in place.

We are looking into this problem.
Our windows crack, shatter. We are looking out of this problem.

These people need iron clad assurances.
We are clad in metal, polyethylene and foam. It is alight.

Steps are being taken to improve safety.
These steps are hot plates. They scald our feet as we run.

Here are the minutes of our last meeting.
Here are the minutes of our last hours.

Those responsible for the tragedy have been replaced.
Those affected by it can't be.

Our condolences rain down on you.
We had no sprinklers to do the same.

All efforts are being made to identify the causes.
Hope vanishes of you ever identifying our corpses.

Now we are ready to listen to your concerns.
Our lips are sealed. Our unheard voices are in your files.

Born to be Airborne

We are the Magnificent Men.
We are Orville and Wilbur,
Bader and Red Baron.
We are Mercury Men
Hermes-helmeted, wax-winged and sun-struck
bound south for the winter.
We are Zeus gliding into intimacy
to a landing strip called Leda.
We are astral projectiles
leaving the launch pad of ourselves.
We are the wearers of wafers of balsa
and coarse canvas collapsing in on ourselves.
We are Amys and Amelias,
Pan and Superman, Ariel and Tinkerbell.
We are wind-lifted and current carried.
We are jet pack and flight map,
magic carpet and Messerschmitt,
balloon-borne and human cannonball
and born to be airborne.
We are dials and pressure gauges,
altitude and attitude
hopping Heath Robinson-ed
with pedal power and propulsion
into two second flight.
We are swallow-dive and swoop,
loop the loop, airship and backflip.
We are 'Lift off Houston'.
We are spotter, prop and crop-duster,
feather and fan-tail.
We are 550cc Royal Enfield
through the wet fence at the cliff edge
and '52 Vincent in Black Lightning free-fall.
We are 50 ways to fly before you die,
8 miles high, pie in the sky.
We are the 51st way to leave your lover
and we sigh, we sigh
like a released handbrake

as we cross oceans and fingers and pray
as we get our fill of full throttle
and are away
up, up and away
always
UP and away.

Under the Influence

Driving too close to a driverless hearse
I rear-ended it, spilled consonants, vowels
and images through the sunroof, air vents,
all the windows. Most broke on impact, spoils

that even the most famished scavenger
would reject, unpalatable roadkill
on frost-rimed tarmac, scattered by no sound.
Even that which was retrievable still

wasn't worth stopping and reversing for:
a worn and sullied image here and there,
brittle as windscreens, an idea or two
in the shape of a wet map, likely to tear.

I'd been fussed and muzzy with others' words;
another's words, my concentration less
than perfect. Such driving was not my style.
The hearse was undented, my carelessness

a warning against following too close
for too long, the cheap smell of 1 star rank,
my cramped fingers on the steering wheel,
a stalled dictionary in the heart's tank.

Teaching My Dog to Swim

Bar *his* collar, *my* shorts,
naked as the day we were born,
we soundlessly split the lake's skin
six-legged, him twelve yards back
already out of his depth, me twelve yards on
comfortably within mine.

Nervy, not really up for it,
the bait of a ball bobbing just out of reach,
he let the lake break about his furred chest,
kept his literal but not metaphorical chin up.

I shuddered my shoulders under,
gasped into the first stroke too stunned cold at first
to check if he was following.
I engaged muscles unused for this for seven years –
the almost age of my dog, the length of the hiatus
from my holidaying abroad.

That evening, at almost seven years old,
my dog gained his first experience of mid-life crisis
in his scrappy semblance of a swimmer,
front paws digging the water,
back claws cheat tiptoeing over stones.

I turned in mercy to him and to land
and remembered that at seven I couldn't swim either.
We tottered the rocky shallows to shore to no applause
and when stark bollock naked – him shaking, me shivering –
a chough strutted by and a launch chugged out of the sun.

We'd sort of done what we came to do. Called it a day.
Reflected on a half job half well done.

The God of Dogs

The God of Dogs knew a thing or two about design;
knew how to make the rolling shoulder's plates
attractive whatever the pace,
how to fuel the head with purpose,
the Dunlop snout with scents unsniffed by us;

knew how to pattern a paw and patent it
so the copycat cat would stop dead in its tracks
and require those tracks made new
copyright of the God of Cats.

The God of Dogs flopped ears or perked them,
lathered His work in fur,
hinged the cocking leg to perfection,
metronomed tails.

To Him goes credit for the wolf cousin and fox
but most for the eyes, the blessed bright eyes
of dogs where the dog lovers melt,
where the world reflects a more finished glow.
To Him give thanks for the warm-scented saints
who walk by and amongst us.

We, dizzy with dyslexia, praise the Son of Dog
for deliverance and he has made a home for us
on the plain of his lolling tongue.
To Him we owe the music of claw tap on wood block,
the complex calligraphy of hair in the shag pile.

Dogs with their valves and varieties
pumped or puffed into being by that God of the air
who fastened those fluid flanks and haunches –
here, the one who punches above his weight;
here, the one who gentles down to size.

God of Dogs, who lies down with the lion and lamb
and outshines them both, what a clever hound you are,
drilled yet disobedient, dropping your depth charge dogs
into a sea of troubles, letting their newly-blown shapes
muscle and fawn and make sense of it all,
make sense of *us* all.

Elvis's Birth Day

Like a thundercrack
in a shotgun shack
in a Southern bed
two Ps in a pod
popped a half hour apart,
one with a wooden heart,
the other new-born-baby-sweet
and bound for Lonely Street.

The stillborn are still born,
clothed in the skin they've worn
for only nine months or so.
They cry neither high nor low
but leave that to those
wrapped in grief, the livings' clothes
of nightdress, pants, shoes, shirt,
who dwell on Earth, not under earth.

Pre-dawn. White Trash room.
Wriggling from the vacant womb
the alive and kicking,
bass note pulse, snare heart ticking,
voice like a hound dog crying
all the time is lying
in his mama's arms,
his sibling cold, his mama warm.

A course set that 8th January –
Graceland. Priceville Cemetery.
Of Tupelo's two twinned children
one's already left the building.
Dawn breaks. Jesse Garon
leaves the stage to Elvis Aron.
A lip curls, a leg twitches,
an axis tips, the world pitches.

Jane's First Harp

arrives with the year's first snow,
settles on the warm side of the window
smelling of Amaretti biscuits.

Sliced light glides between strings
and its ribbed shadow shudders
as it's plucked and raked

until, a December week on,
the lowest sun of solstice
can no longer find it.

On the cold side of the glass
snow shreds down as if God
or St. Cecilia were planing the sky,

letting the shavings, like notes
from a vanilla-scented harp,
fall where they may.

At such times are contracts sealed:
earth and sky, wood and string,
music and light.

The sun moves behind hedge and elm.
From a low energy bulb a trembling grid
ripples Jane's face, crosses her heart.

Survival Techniques

never go in without your skin
keep the nerves and the veins and the muscles within
make sure the knee bone connects to the shin
never back out if you can't get back in
lead with your left, not with your chin
watch for the welt where the wounds begin
don't be the kin be the next of kin
never go in without your skin

never go in without your skin
forget where you're going but not where you've been
make sure that your genned up and genuine
drop a coin for the guy with the mandolin
make room for the fat, make food for the thin
keep what you lose, share what you win
give brains to the straw man, heart to the tin
never go in without your skin

never go in without your skin
don't try to walk before you can swim
check out the surface, watch for the fin
when entering church, when singing a hymn
keep your eye on the service, watch for the spin
measure the depth and the width of your sin
you'll not see nothing like the mighty quinn
never go in without your skin

never go in without your skin
remember the day you should put out your bin
always begin the beguine with begin
make the right noises, keep down the din
don't try to split the yang from the yin
don't be madonna, be marilyn
go out like a light, go in like flynn
never go in without your skin

never go in without your skin
don't pick a fight with a paladin
don't pick a fight at all, pick a mandolin
be careful with nitroglycerin
don't put out a bushfire with paraffin
never light up in a zeppelin
watch which you throw when you pull out the pin
never go in without your skin

never go in without your skin
don't ride a bike in a crinoline
ask miranda if she remembers an inn
take out the ice and the juice from the gin
don't confuse mickey mouse with mickey finn
don't step on a nail in a moccasin
don't keep a shrew with a peregrine
never go in without your skin

never go in without your skin
or make original sin your origin
know which is yourself and which is your twin
watch out for the bull in the bulletin
check out the checks on a harlequin
be sure what you mean by discipline
buy your best bed from a bedouin
never go in without your skin

never go in without your skin
don't bodybuild on insulin
make sure that you gel with the gelatin
check that it does what it says on the tin
remember to take the right vitamin
don't play pool with a javelin
don't disappear without taking your grin
never go in without your skin

never go in without your skin
don't make attachments you can't unpin
be sure what you mean by feminine
don't trust a hero or heroine
try to be sweet but not saccharin
if you want to be thought of as masculine
be a man my son not a mannequin
never go in without your skin

never go out without a shout
go raging or gentle or thrashing about
you start out with breath and you end up with nowt
be a good girl and a good boy scout
devote half your life just to being devout
ne'er cast a clout until may is out
take heed what I say, believe what I spout
although I don't know what I'm talking about
never go in without your skin
never go out without your doubt
never go out without your doubt

God's Library

as you might imagine, is extensive,
shelves so high that either ladders or wings
are required to select those bindings
placed highest. The subject matter – exhaustive,
though somewhat predictable, all the books
there written, as it were, by God Himself.
But nothing lowbrow, mind. Upon each shelf
marked G – G, His own strange stories. Look!
Here's one about a gardener who grows sin,
another on a flood, one about nets cast.
Each one with its own particular twist;
each worth taking out and taking out again.
Check this out: up there God claims they're all by Him
yet down here man has put his stamp on them.

Bored Games

At times, when darkness
wasn't enough of a mask,
they shelled out for others.

He always let her have first choice
when it came to bedroom toys
so did not complain

when his, simple and shapeless,
went up against her 'Mardi Gras special',
card to stiffened card.

It was harder to kiss
but different, though every other touch
was familiar and unimpeded.

He lost interest at last
when her glitter-scattered mask
became less concubine

with the lights turned up,
more death's head moth –
dead eyes in the cut-outs.

Inheritance

Our Aunt left us a cottage.
She didn't mean to but she did.
Slate it was. Neo-Gothic with chimneys like turrets,
gargoyles in her likeness
and a gash of gate where the fence gave out.
You couldn't have shifted that place
for love nor money
and there was sod all of either
in its low rooms when we got it.

Everything about it was her: its mean light
and narrow views, its fittings that didn't.
We poured nowt back into it but resentment,
shuttered it up the long winter long,
Havishamed her memory in the gloomiest room
she left us, stuck the Viewing by Appointment pitch
on a sign too big for its boots on an angled pole
in the given up ghost garden.

Empty, you'd think you saw smoke
shimmying out of the chimneys
but it's the light round here plays tricks;
something to do with steam on slow drying slate,
weather fronts and sea air. It's a mystery to us,
like the way it was left. To us, I mean.
The cottage, I mean. Not like her that.
Come Spring we think we hear the eaves dropping
the way she would through the bedroom floor;
open the windows wide the way her heart wouldn't.

Act of God

After a particularly bad night's sleep
God awoke and decided to de-bone the ocean:
cod, kipper, halibut and tench,
drowned fisherman, sailorman, ferryman and child,
whalebone, wishbone, collarbone, jaw.
He boned bloater, swimmer and flatfish; went in
for blunt shin and feathered spine,
nicked into gills, shredded tails,
bored through nostril and socket
and close-cleaned the marine biologist
who'd got too close to his work; made no distinction
between sea visitor and lodger, accident and suicide –
skewered and skewed until the scaled and skinny husks
whistled in the hollows of the sea.

Being God, it didn't take long –
seven seas stripped in as many seconds,
giving the reef something soft to bite into
before the ribbed surf retreated as the tide turned,
the half skull of a cloud-cleaved moon
above the funnelled out and filleted sea.
When waning, net and talon, beak and hook
caught and brought up an easier feed
to be taken at the table or on the wing.
The dead's scaffolding sank to the sea-bed
and the blind, bulb-eyed, bug-eyed and boneless
bobbed and dodged under a hail of white shrapnel.

Now the kings of the deep are the spineless
where squid, ray and jellyfish rule and reign,
until God, done with such contrariness,
will reinstate raw order, knuckle down,
put the wet world to some sort of rights again.
For us it would be a bother but God, being God,
takes such tasks in His universe-spanning stride.
Whether extracting bone from the living or
plugging it back into the dead, this is what he does.

In temper or boredom, as warning or whim, this is what he does.
These are the tricks of His trade, we the sharks, crabs,
the hapless, fighting tooth and claw to understand.

Great Authors Strike Great Poses

Stevenson – blazered, all almond eyes,
perfect moustache and tie adrift,
slouching with a body's seaboard lilt.
Whitman – workmanlike, wafered between
the leaves of grass on a green marbled cover
and ninety-five printed pages, fist on hip,
hand in pocket, open-neck shirt, beard,
raised bring-it-on eyebrow, hat and handsome head tilt.
Dodgson – delicately boyish at thirty-two,
his right androgynous hand to his dreamy head,
the other poised by a watch-chain. Or, similarly dreamy,
absently cleaning a camera lens or dropping
pensive eyes onto a work in progress.

Did they all already know – the established and the obscure –
about immortality; assuredly convey a 'capture all this'
attitude before the hand-held light exploded?
'Remember me this way', says Keats
pushing his knuckles into his right cheek
and C.A. Brown catches in sketch
what the camera, itching for invention, can't:
a shy eye, two years shy of death,
and (the pencil never lies) a two-buttoned cuff
high on the sleeve, tight curls above a face
on which, at least then, no lines had been written.

Remembering My Lines

Hood remembered twice in his first line;
Rossetti only once. That much, at least,
I know. I knew their names as well as my own –
still do some days. It's yours I forget most.
"Son!" you say. "Mum, I'm your son. Remember?"
I recall someone younger in your place.
A difficult birth he was. December
baby like his Dad. Something in your face
seems familiar, though. Poems I read him –
that son you say you are. 'David' was it?
Things blur sometimes. My memory turns dim.
The verse comes back, though; a poem does it.
A sonnet is sixteen lines in number.
No, not sixteen. Fourteen. I remember.

The Bone Carpenters

The Bone Carpenters chiselled hard,
chiselled hard at beast and breastbone,
shin and shiny calcium, cold chalk,
they sold talk as cheap as sleep unslept
that's kept in the venetian of a ribcage,
alert to the still skeleton's mobilised
socket that rocks like a crocked athlete
in the swagger of shadow and light,
alert as ones undazed by the grey dust
thrown down in the brown foundry
of the Bone Carpenters' workshop.

The Bone Carpenters plane the bones
of the cold, the stiff, life's spent cartridges,
those with hearts done and fired dry,
those cartilages powdering under failed skin,
silent as unspoken sin and thin as a Bone Carpenter.
All night they hammer and mallet at it,
hammer and tongs, tongues jawing till dawn
about the bones they've drawn and quartered,
alter all of the town's dead images
from the caught and slaughtered,
scrape and sculpt those fixtures into paving stones,
telephones (that old 'dog and bone'), turn a war zone
into a factory of art, start to work on each new shape,
each misshape, reconstruct the solid and crumbled
until they've assembled match tins, fire guards,
bone yards of everyday objects no-one will object to.

All day, at rest, the Bone Carpenters dream
their milky dreams of healthy bones picked clean,
licked clean of marrow and skin,
borrow night's cutters, carvers and cleavers,
toil blissfully through a full day's sleep,
keep that thought on waking,
on making their merry way to their factory.

And after decades of this graft with no-one new
to draft in, no apprentice ready to be skilled
in the art, the craft of the fresh and freshly killed,
all potential candidates call-centred
or hard-lining on hard drives, the Bone Carpenters
die off, feed the stock but starve the work force,
live on in vase, pen, handle and playpen
but do nothing more. And then one day
when the last Bone Carpenter is gone,
whilst there'll be more, much more to do,
nothing more will be done.

Dream Twister

So where *have* you been, our blue-eyed son?
Your answer likely to be shrugs, sighs or silence,
so who knows where your spectacular self sprang from,
where this unspectacular boy, dusted with iron ore
and Minnesota manners found Bob Dylan,
baptised him with the oil of imagined freight trains
and pointed him south down Highway 61?

And what did you see and shape universal
from a New York blizzard?
Something so blazingly bright that we were blinded
and missed it until you showed it us, told it us
in words, some light, some so heavy it's a miracle
they managed flight before snagging
on your barbed mind then loosening into song?

And what did you hear in the rhythm of rail, chink of coffee cup,
in the whippoorwill and wail of Hank Williams
that no-one else could hear as clearly?
What coiled and wound in your ear,
wormed in and mutated into masterpiece?
What is the sound that stirs a cypher into shaman and sage?

And who did you meet along the way,
those bards, bowdlerises and balladeers of the street?
The ghosts of Guthrie's own past and Guthrie himself?
The hell hound that stalked Robert Johnson?
The spirits of Grant and Lee at Appomattox?
The phantom pilgrim, Indian and slave?

And what now? What now, our blue-eyed son,
best surviving navigator of Rimbaud's drunken boat,
most articulate gnarled nightingale of the poetry of song?
Dream shatterer, keeper of no-one's flame, what'll you do now,
now that we all know your song well before you start singing?
Still that same question: what'll you do now?

Touchdown

Abandoned village - Tsougria, Greece

Here is where the birds come down.
They belly up in tin baths, slick as seals,
hang their talisman claws from ceiling hooks,
doze relentlessly dead in the undergrowth
to a future of feather and bone.

They hood down wet between walls
and are brick dusted and blown bone dry
amongst the remnants of picnics:
a bottle of sugar and wasps,
a pizza, 40 minutes eaten, with
a second-hand shadow ticking over what's left.

In here, the bone white x-ray of moonlight
through shutters is on the shredded curtain.
Out there, the tiny bows of swallows
above the fetid lake; the feathers of the dead
quivering with blackfly on the marshes;
the sea's heavy undertow in the still blue day.

Request

I want a poem that anyone can sing
whether or not they can carry a tune,
a poem that holds back seas, shifts continents,
shelters you from rain.
I want a poem of mass construction
that outguns every other poem that opposes it,
one whose title is a flag of all nations.
I want a poem that's yet to be invented,
a many striking match of a poem,
an inextinguishable flame of syllables and sounds.
I want words that stitch wounds, clear consciences, salve sores,
ones that mend broken hearts, find lost souls,
bust the case wide open.
I want a poem that pollutes poison,
one that injects a serum of blue blood and red socialism
into veins of every persuasion to make them royally proud.
I want a poem that tames tearaways or tears after them,
a poem that breaks all the wrong and right rules,
a poem without manifesto or promise.
I want a poem that breastfeeds on public transport,
urinates outside pay-to-use toilets, pays its way at the bar.
I want a poem with a left-hand drive and an automatic shift,
one that illegally passes on its ticket at pay and display car parks.
I want a poem that starts first time in cold weather
and that drives when I drink.
I want a poem that can meet with Triumph and Disaster
and treat those two imposters as just lines from Kipling.
I want a poem that strips bark, lightens dark
makes a covenant – an ark for couplets to board.
I want a poem that mates with itself, a double rainbow of a poem,
a double echo, a double exposure, a double de clutch of a poem
that doubles for something else.
I want a poem that circles its wagons and invites the Indians in,
one that gets the weather forecast right,
one that can tell fortunes but won't.
I want a poem that's called 'Archibald' for no apparent reason,
a poem called 'Autumn' that isn't about it.

I want a poem that promises to pay the bearer then reneges.
I want a white tablecloth of a poem pulled out
from under fine china.
I want a poem a whale would swallow, one for Jonah
to read when things get slow in there.
I want a poem with no make-up but with lipstick on its collar.
I want an informal, open-necked poem,
one that behaves badly in polite society.
I want a poem that talks you down off the ledge,
that talks you into life, that talks and says something
or says nothing beautifully.
I want a poem that gives hearing to the blind
and sight to the deaf.
I want a poem that unblocks clogged arteries
and performs open heart surgery.
I want a page poem, stage poem, sad poem, glad poem,
a poem of therapy, majesty, apathy,
of anything I want it to be.
I want a poem that does all/some/none of these things.
Like a magician needs his tricks,
a footballer needs his kicks,
a school kid needs his ticks,
a musician needs his licks,
an addict needs his fix,
I need a poem.
I want a poem.
Now.

The Grave Garden

At first there was dry weather work,
a little light weeding, a little heavy,
soiled knees and dropped seeds,
a one-way conversation with the cat
but then she found another thing to do –
something outside that the rain
couldn't handle – and took to that.

It was close work – her house, third left
in a row of nine that fronted the churchyard;
close work – her hand tipping the can less than a foot
above each puffed plot, each grassed plot,
the water arcing from the plastic rose delicately
as a tongue arches to melt a wafer of bread.

What rose were bones: knuckles, shins, the room
that once housed the mouth, the nose, the eyes.
She liked it best when they cracked dry earth – a toe
opening the crust like a chick from a shell –
but the surfacings through sodden soil would do.
The growth was quicker than the weeds.

Other stuff died. Whilst sprays and bouquets
perished into stalks against the headstones
she watched digit become hand, hand become wrist,
wrist become forearm, elbow and arm.
Elsewhere, legs sprouted, jaws thrust, chins jutted,
bodies took shape and stopped and slept on earth's bed.

They were there all Summer, naked of flesh,
but no neighbour complained; not one dissenting voice.
After all, what harm was there in it? No fuss. No smell.
No sound but for the wind that played the cavity
of a skull like a conch; the ribs like a harp.
They were all gone by Autumn anyway, sunk back
into wood or soil's remembered shape of them.

Deaths by the dozen by their doorsteps
yet all Summer her neighbours had passed her
and no comment; passed her on their way
between the risen bones and tombstones to the church;
passed as she tendered to that garden of graves
as if they saw nothing but her seeing nothing.

Nobody had complained; not one dissenting voice.
No-one even remarked. She liked that,
liked them – her 'minding my own business' neighbours
who knew when to be discreet. She turned to other things,
spent the winter on wicker work, a little light reading,
a little heavy, a one-way conversation with the cat.

Wrestlers and Meadow Flowers

Put these boys under delicate decoration
until they wear these petals like scales.
Let their violence turn fancy,
their skins' discipline grow nature-wild.

Even unshowered they were too soft
for their sport, too tentative in their touch;
their unenthusiastic eyes too distracted
and dreamy for their task.

Better buried here, a vase's width between them,
petalled heads, unmauled muscles
smothered in small flowers
turning their tautness flimsy.

But let the badge of each bloom,
be a new wound blossoming.
For the sake of their pride
at least let them have that.

X-ray finds a Van Gogh painting of wrestlers beneath his painting 'Still life with meadow flowers and roses'

Occasional Table

but occasionally not. Once
in a piney dream of summer rain
and oleander it flattened
and became a Huck Finn raft
muddied up on the banks of the Mississippi;
another time became a copy
of the New York Times covering
the hatched tables under it.

Most ambitiously, on one occasion
it lifted its hinged flaps and flew,
glided four times around the dining room
unsettling nothing but the dust
under its landing gear. Later
that day when its owners had risen,
it was hangered under a bookshelf
whilst the runway was cleaned.

And once, in the sweetest dream of all,
it timbered up into its former self
and its trunk hunkered down amongst others,
no sound of buzzsaw or axe.
It awoke, yawned and stretched arms
full of leaves no longer of wood,
held nests no longer of tables.

Love & Crossbones

There's nothing that more disappoints
than love found wanting, love that won't

prove faithful to the bitter end
no matter to which cross it's pinned,

that once it's fixed, hung out to dry,
always either lies or dies.

The lovers who had *thought* love died
discovered it had been shanghaied

and over two crossed skull-less bones
a heart thought dead was deftly sewn

and threaded through the weave and weft
by men content with what was left

till etched out on a bleached-out rag
they raised it on a half-mast flag.

And there it flew, both night and day,
a compass pointing out The Way,

an anchor in the sailors' drift,
a code by which their lives were lived.

The heart stayed true, the bones held fast.
No blood or splinters left that mast,

not one shred of flag was lost,
not one bargain double-crossed.

A while, despite the crosswind's blast,
it hung there from that steady mast

until that day when ragged, torn
it came away in tempest storm.

And when the storm was spent and through
this weathered, broken-hearted crew

stood over where the crossbones crossed
and recognised the heart was lost.

They crossed their own hearts, bowed and then
vowed loud it would be found again.

One day the vessel reached the shore
(The heart or ship? No-one was sure.)

but in some misshape, run aground
on blasted, parched, unholy land

the capsized love spilled on the beach
and scattered from the sailors' reach

where it was found and carried off
by one portentous lovesick dove

who took the heart the crew had lost
and nailed it to a hilltop cross.

Wolves dragged it down as thunder cracked.
It hid in stone. The stone rolled back.

The thunder rolled. The heart rolled too,
back to the ship, the heartsick crew,

unseen by them. Convinced they'd failed
they lifted anchor, hoisted sail.

The heartless flag lay on the deck.
They tied it round the lifeless neck –

at just the point the crossbones cross —
of some abandoned albatross

the captain shot the day before
they'd pulled out from that wretched shore.

The weather turned from mild to mean
and evermore that heart, unseen,

rocked upon that curséd ship.
Successive crews in blind worship

would hear it from some distant mount
or glimpse it as a ghostly print

upon the shroud of that worn cloth
that once had been a flag with both

the heart and bones of life and death,
a martyr's badge, a lover's breath.

Snake Belt

As a kid, the knack of keeping your cool
or kecks up was to make it eat its own tail.
It stretched, catapult-tense, through the vertebrae
of loops on my jeans and its silver motif
was angled and anchored at the stomach's pit.

My mother, who writhed like a snake at the sight
of the real thing, who couldn't even stomach one
tanked in the TV, who was afraid of the very thought
replaced my belts as they frayed without a flinch,
each new one banded in stripes the old had forgotten.

The depth of her courage escaped me as I slithered them in place.
Only now do I wonder which of us wasn't paying attention;
which of us truly understood the world as it was.

Selective Memory

One fine spring day
my brother gave me the gift of electricity:
a fire engine red, catalogue-bought guitar
his son had forgotten to learn. I tried it on.
Through the mesh of a damaged amp
cack-handed chords popped and spat
in the sunlit lounge of his Somerset house
and all my soft fingers complained.
The birds and my brother flew north.

Tell it like this:

One stormy winter's night
my brother hauled me horizontal
to the ceiling of a shadowy castle,
a gnarled branch across my chest.
A lever was yanked, the roof rolled back
and the lightning fizzed.
I descended in a blaze of purple haze,
landed feet apart with the reshaped wood shouldered,
squeezed with my left hand, raked with my right
and the room was filled with creation.
From the rafters bats hung on every note,
joined my brother in one astonished voice.
It's alive! they cried. *It's alive!*

Me and George VI

They buried him the day before I was born.
I remark on this fact, making no claim
for reincarnation – his casket, borne
on broad, important shoulders gently lain
in soil less than 24 hours before I'm hauled
from womb to air. But consider this, when
exactly, at death or burial, do souls
depart the shell; cross from king to common man?
I don't know at what speed spirits teleport
but fast enough, I'm sure, to go from London
to Stepping Hill Hospital, Stockport,
Maternity Ward 2, bed number 1.
Just saying, stranger things happen at sea.
(Or is that 'worse' things?) Anyway, could be.

Blue Eyes

Just yesterday in humankind's time-line,
six to ten thousand years of blue-eyed babes –
Paul Newman, Bob Dylan, *My Blue-Eyed Jane* –
were launched by one who bucked the trend of green

and brown. He or she, through Melanin's rum
behaviour, lit two bright pilot lights
steady enough to fire up the sight
of all the cold-eyed and glamour-eyed to come.

And with them – poems and songs without number,
stuffed with similes of sky, sea and sapphire.
Even moons took on their hue; words inspired
by beauty, love, longing, sadness, wonder.

Who, blessed with such eyes, would wish to trade this gift
of blue for hazel, emerald green or brown?
Even paled with age in faces grown
tired of compliment, their appeal is long-lived.

The reindeer, though, its two eyes in two minds, shows
golden brown in the summer months but glows
blue in winter. Reflected light scatters.
What care they for ornament, flash or show?
When it's eat or be eaten, blue matters.

Skin on Skin

You could say we're close, my sister and me.
We have our moments; know what I mean?
But a kick from her once when we were fifteen
was one too many. One down, both down, see?

Black moods though, harsh words, angry exchanges.
But nothing violent, mind. We're sisters, see?
Flesh and blood. Two of a kind, her and me.
They talk separation. That won't change us.

True, we've never looked at each other
but the same tingle that runs down her spine
never fails to course the length of mine.
We've blood thicker than most; flesh still closer.

She says nothing behind my back I don't hear.
We have warm hearts. When sadness turns them colder
we angle arms like wings over our shoulders,
cup palms on each other's cheek; catch a tear.

Rags and Tatters

Ditch-muddy, bloody and dead
see them ghost in, all in their rags and tatters.
Behind the steel drone
and the squeal of finger on fret,
between the clamped neck,
triangular D and arched G,
within the pick, pluck and strum
all those Mattys and Donalds,
Delias, Pollys,
Omies and Geordies,
brothers, sons, cowards and lords;
all of those luckless maidens,
barely heavy with child and with 'Mercy!'
glazed on their lips for eternity
are in at this phantom roll call.

From the sacked castles of shadowy kings
and the shallow-hearted lovers of shallower graves
to the places of poacher and chancer,
see all those swung souls who are hung in song,
in courtyard, from yardarm and in lonely upstairs room,
suddenly find their feet and pad in.
And watch those scorned in love,
scorched by lust, burst from their restless place,
headless or sightless or wounded in spirit,
briars twisting in their barbed hearts,
beaten swords in their breasts;
watch them come, clay cold and shivering,
to search for their winding sheets.

In a world of recurring,
where the curses number 7
and the babies, wishes and turns, always 3;
where hair is as black as ravens
and daggers forever silver,
they confess and complain;
roll out their lyric laments.

Where now are their butcher boys,
their Daemon lovers; where now
the long black veil drawn over the sorry tale?
Where in the throb of bodhran,
the reel of fiddle, the raked chord;
where in the nightingale note are they headed?

From Bruton Town to Bohenny,
with the hills of Heaven or Hellfire
bathing or torching their horizons,
here they are assembled,
all in their rags and tatters,
golden locks and jet-black curls
ribboned with scarlet,
their milk white steeds ghosting away from them,
their tiny boats sunk beyond refrain,
their murderers' hands turned to geese in a grey sky.

Offerings

Feed the air
anything winged by nature
that has a desire for flight.

Feed the water
with its gravity-defying self
running out of steam.

Feed the earth
the seeds of the living,
the seeds of the dead.
Let it keep what it needs,
give up what it offers.

Feed the fire
with the air for its dances,
the water for its slumbers,
the earth's alternate wood and soil
for its curtain call.

Offer us life.
Name us with water.
Let us breathe, drink, walk,
be warmed and illuminated.

Bury us in earth.
Scatter us in air.
Burn us in fire.

We rise like steam,
fall as rain,
are collected for new namings.

Off Track

I was told I'd find things
in this Devil-forsaken wood
and my expectations rose to the treetops.
None of them were here –
none of the things I imagined:
not Barrie's lost boys
dreaming deathly of nannies and nurseries,
not Shangri La, Nirvana or Byzantium,
not Bigfoot moving as shadow through shadow itself,
no Holy Grail leaking its lifeblood
into the vermin's last supper of the day –
no echo of this from a crucifix tree,
no Lord Lucan leafed out in copper for modesty's sake,
no Jimmy Hoffa in cashmere or concrete,
no survivors of Roswell
limping saucer-eyed through the undergrowth.
Betty Page and Salinger weren't here
nor were Kennedy's killers.
I didn't even achieve the obvious
and find myself;
not without doubling back,
measuring my footprints,
picking up my scent,
reading this through a second time.

Dragon Deaths

It's what we want, what we're after,
to rise new-scaled from the grave,
hot-breathed and wing-flexed for another go.

It's the mound of gold we covet,
that we wrap lustful tails and tongues around,
what we wish and hiss for:

to fall from the great height of a place thought lost,
to drop from the cave of death's womb
into the arms of a brand new shadow,

to board immortality's carousel,
for someone to stoke our bellies' furnace,
raise smoke from ash and fire from smoke,

to rescue us from one worm
and make another of our selves,
to tear that veil with fresh green talons

and fork lightning from our tongues.
This time we swear we'll more than scorch the scenery.
This time we will truly make our mark.

Out of Order

In the papers we die alphabetically.
In the bible too, Abel queue jumping his father
by nine hundred years or more.
And alphabetically, electorally we turn eighteen
then yellow page what we're up to from A-Z.

We live recorded linear lives but, off the record, fuck up –
the first becoming last (or ninth or third),
don't hatch or match in order but shuffle our coils
even before we shuffle them off, gasp to no-one's last
but our own, peg out out of sequence, slough off out of sync.

This is news to no-one but the tidy, the ordered and confused.
Even 'Zabowski, the Optimist', knows the next could be him.
Mark this: Cain didn't break the law,
he tried to live to the letter of it;
broke nothing but his brother's skull in the process.

Burying Alice

Toys call from the floor but she's paint to apply –
not to her picture books, to her lips and her eyes.
What the hell do we sell her and what does she buy?
Is that a schoolbag or handbag she carries?
Burying Alice.

She's lightweight, she's jailbait, she's prime for a pass.
She's poised for the pill and she'll give all she has.
She's trapped at the mirror, can't pass through the glass
and the rabbit hole's now an abyss
for Alice.

Her heroines are cheap and she's heroin thin.
She's reality T.V. conditioned and dim,
says "He's sleeping with her, she's sleeping with him".
Is it her or us who's embarrassed
when burying Alice?

She's dressed for the kill and she'd kill for a drag.
She's a Barbie doll babe and a wannabe wag
and the kind call her cute and the cruel call her slag
and she's growing from London to Paris
without Alice.

We act like this somehow was all unforeseen
yet gave her the tools and the ways and the means
to miss out on the land of betwixt and between
and replace it with knowing and malice
towards Alice.

She's in at the deep end and can't really swim,
sees a flash of blue dress at the rabbit hole's rim
but the chance of her getting back down there is slim
with the weight of the world that she carries.
Unlike Alice.

Viewing Platform, Delabole Slate Quarry

A drop of Zakynthos in this tiered Cornish landscape;
a lagoon of pure Greece in the quarry's raw wind.
In the shuffles of slate Crinoid, Pecten and Asteroid
have fossilised, but I know nothing of them save their names.
Nor do I know the Spirifer - the 'Delabole Butterfly',
webbed, ambered and landlocked; only that he/she
is a bi-valved shellfish whose twin-barrelled gills
have breathed in, but not out, for centuries.
At dusk the day's drooping light mobilises the benches,
makes escalators of the slatted steps. The lagoon
turns to battery acid as the Mediterranean corrodes.

Not Just for Weddings

Four years before paddle steaming
out of this world into the next, Mark Twain
donned linen as pure and snow white as snow,
every day – white slippers, socks and shirt,
white overcoat for the out, white dressing gown for the in.

Seems now, and maybe then, no-one knows or agrees
why this sinner chose the colour of intense light
to prepare for the deepest dark; why he asked
to be laid out in the favoured shade of angels;
why, under the generous froth of his moustache,
he stayed taciturn whenever talk would turn
to matters of colour, muttering only of hygiene
and a penchant in winter for dress of 'unseasonable cloths'.

A cool look, though, in both senses:
brown and white patent leather shoes, cashmere suit,
felt hat, corncob pipe plugged in a face
as ruddy as the Mississippi River at sundown.
When you're old, bath-chaired and stylish
there's no room for pathos. Mark Twain is a stern turn
in almost every Tintype, Daguerreotype and Ambrotype
we ever see but never more so than when taking the last suns
he'll ever take, ready to go out with the comet he came in with.

It was on a day that one day became my birthday
that Edison clocked him in Redding, Connecticut
sailor-gaiting round the corner of Stormfield,
lapping the house in clothes as white as a picket fence.
Then, seated at white china tea with his daughters
while the film (the film!) bleaches with time,
Twain talking of who-knows-what but no doubt brilliantly,
silently requesting more tea, or coffee,
black maybe, more probably white.

The next year, true to his name, they buried him
about two fathoms deep, no Heaven or Hell to claim him,
a white rash of snowdrops sprouting above him,
pine, earth and all competition – then and to follow – below.

Bateman, Skinner and Withers

Bateman would have it that this flower,
the last frail spoke in Creation's wheel,
turned a soon flawed Earth to beauty.

Mania is not too strong a word
for what he henceforth summons:
cargoes of Eden brought in on fashion's tide.

George Ure Skinner sees the spray of his life
open, blossom. He gathers a generous bouquet,
a shipment of seed and plant unseen,

turns from bird and bug to orchid,
picks, plucks and boxes for 35 years.
Caught between ships, he Solomon Grundys –

queasy on Monday, sick on Tuesday,
dead on Wednesday – out of this world
and Panama by the swiftest route left to him.

He's recalled in Mrs. Withers' delicate
tracery: the colour of his fever
etched in the flowers of Oncidium,

its leaves the sleek wings of some
Guatemalan bird he'd once ushered
to England in the French cannons' wake.

At Least Two Litres a Day

First a sip
slipped across the tongue
and swallowed like a forced apology
then a swill, a gulp, a long draught.

I moved from delicate blue thimble
to cupped palm
via glass, tumbler and jug
to jug-eared pitcher
tilted on straining, rivered arms
to my lips.

My wet tongue
learned well the incantation –
Buxton, Evian, Pellegrino and tap,
filtered and sparkling –
until, in less than the time drowning takes,
I'd topped up my 10% or more
and was awash with well-being;
tongue no longer able to rudder the flow
down my broken dam throat.

And that was it really.
I'd thought myself the vessel, the craft
taking on water, willingly sinking
until I capsized into myself;
knew then I was river, lake and stream,
an entire ocean of me. I saw a world unpolluted,
an albatross unharmed.

Resurrection

So behold the clinching trick:
the mortal coil not so much sloughed off as electrified.
Unsnagged by nail or thorn he thrums with fiery charge.

An angel lands, sparking on shaking ground,
trembles the sentries and jump-starts the dead.
To some, more than just day begins to dawn.

And do we dream this burning sprite,
this rolled stone, these bewildered women,
the multitude drying their eyes on the rags of rumour?

The air fizzes with possibilities –
a man of spent breath abroad in an electric dawn,
broken-bread body mended, wine-coloured blood unspilled.

Blessings

God bless the living and God bless the dead
the out of our hands and the out of their heads
the easily caught and the easily led
and God bless Elvis

God bless the artists whose art can unnerve us
but God bless the knackered, no-hopers and nervous
God bless the sense of a National Health Service
and God bless Elvis

God bless the stricken and God bless the struck
the down in the dumps and the down on their luck
God bless the shaken and God bless the shook
and God bless Elvis

God bless Hank Williams and God bless Woody
God bless Eddie and God bless Buddy
God bless the gone and the bruised and the bloody
God bless Elvis

God bless John and God bless Paul
God bless the long and the short and the tall
Bless 'em all, bless 'em all, bless 'em all, bless 'em all
and God bless Elvis

God bless the losers and God bless the lost
God bless the matter and God bless the ghost
God bless the last train that leaves for the coast
and God bless Elvis

God bless the hammer and God bless the nail
God bless the failing and bless those that fail
God bless the ones who can rise up and rail
God bless Elvis

God bless the searching and searched for and such
God bless the toucher and God bless the touched
God bless the lonely who long for as much
and God bless Elvis

God bless the ones who fought to be free
Bless Bessie Smith and Muhammad Ali
God bless America and please God bless me
and God bless Elvis

God bless our fingers and God bless our toes
God bless the people who have none of those
God bless the freezing and bless all who froze
and God bless Elvis

God bless the kisser and God bless the kissed
and God bless God if God really exists
God bless the missing and God bless the missed
God bless Elvis

God bless the caring, the kind, the unselfish
God bless the lonely as nobody else is
God bless the power of the pulse and the pelvis
God bless

God bless the serious, God bless the flip
God bless the voice and God bless the hip
God bless the curl of the hair and the lip
God bless Elvis

God bless his Mama and God bless his twin
God bless the light that he left us all in
God bless us and God bless him
God bless Elvis

Lightning Source UK Ltd.
Milton Keynes UK
UKHW04f0243041018
329891UK00001B/91/P